# H.E.R.

## SINGER, SONGWRITER, AND GUITARIST

BY DORIS EDWARDS

Essential Library

An Imprint of Abdo Publishing
abdobooks.com

# ABDOBOOKS.COM

Published by Abdo Publishing, a division of ABDO, PO Box 398166, Minneapolis, Minnesota 55439. Copyright © 2022 by Abdo Consulting Group, Inc. International copyrights reserved in all countries. No part of this book may be reproduced in any form without written permission from the publisher. Essential Library™ is a trademark and logo of Abdo Publishing.

Printed in the United States of America, North Mankato, Minnesota.
102021
012022

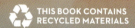

Cover Photo: Rich Fury/Getty Images for dcp/Getty Images Entertainment/Getty Images
Interior Photos: Matt Sayles/Invision/AP Images, 4–5, 57; Lucy Nicholson/Reuters/Newscom, 6; Mike Blake/Reuters/Newscom, 9; Dan MacMedan/Getty Images Entertainment/Getty Images, 12; Kathy Hutchins/Shutterstock Images, 14; Tonya Wise/London Entertainment/Splash/Newscom, 16; Shutterstock Images, 18, 45, 83; Ralph Dominguez/MediaPunch/IPX/AP Images, 21; iStockphoto, 23; Everett Collection/Shutterstock Images, 25; A. M. Parks/iPhoto Inc./Newscom, 26; Matt Sayles/AP Images, 28, 35; Fred Prouser/Reuters/Newscom, 29; Ralf Liebhold/Shutterstock Images, 31; Frank Micelotta/Invsion/AP Images, 33; Richard Shotwell/Invision/AP Images, 36, 63; Chris Pizzello/Invision/AP Images, 38–39, 95, 96–97; Earl Gibson III/Getty Images for ASCAP/Getty Images Entertainment/Getty Images, 40; Daniel DeSlover/Zuma Press/Newscom, 43; Xavier Collin/Image Press Agency/Sipa USA/Newscom, 47; Victoria Will/Invision/AP Images, 50; JLJ/ZOJ/JLN Photography/Wenn/Newscom, 55; Jamie Lamor Thompson/Shutterstock Images, 58; Charles Sykes/Invision/AP Images, 60; Image Press Agency/Sipa USA/Newscom, 66–67; Xavier Collin/Image Press Agency/Mega/Newscom, 70; Featureflash Photo Agency/Shutterstock Images, 72; Amy Harris/Invision/AP Images, 75; Delmiro Junior/Shutterstock Images, 77; Donald Traill/Invision/AP Images, 78, 81; Lev Radin/Shutterstock Images, 82; Brian Friedman/Shutterstock Images, 84–85; Sthanlee B. Mirador/Sipa USA/AP Images, 86; Earl Gibson III/AP Images, 88; Invision/Television Academy/AP Images, 91; Ric Tapia/AP Images, 94

Editor: Arnold Ringstad
Series Designer: Laura Graphenteen

## LIBRARY OF CONGRESS CONTROL NUMBER: 2021941117
## PUBLISHER'S CATALOGING-IN-PUBLICATION DATA

Names: Edwards, Doris, author.
Title: H.E.R.: singer, songwriter, and guitarist / by Doris Edwards.
Other title: singer, songwriter, and guitarist
Description: Minneapolis, Minnesota : Abdo Publishing, 2022 | Series: Hip-hop artists | Includes online resources and index.
Identifiers: ISBN 9781532196157 (lib. bdg.) | ISBN 9781098217969 (ebook)
Subjects: LCSH: H.E.R. (Gabriella Wilson), 1997---Juvenile literature. | Rap musicians--United States--Biography--Juvenile literature. | Rap (Music)--Juvenile literature. | Lyricists--Biography--Juvenile literature.
Classification: DDC 782.421649--dc23

# CONTENTS

# Chapter ONE

# A NIGHT TO REMEMBER

February 10, 2019, was a night musicians across America had been waiting for. The 61st Grammy Awards, the music industry's most celebrated event of the year, had finally arrived. Performers, reporters, and fans were eager to see how the evening would unfold.

The stakes were high. Big powerhouses such as Drake, Kacey Musgraves, and Childish Gambino were nominated for some of the night's most prestigious awards. Media outlets such as Vulture and Pitchfork were betting on Cardi B to take home a pile of gold trophies, including Record of the Year for "I Like It." *Vanity Fair* projected that "Shallow" by Lady Gaga and Bradley Cooper would take the prize for Song of the Year. But there was also one notable new star that everyone seemed to be curious

H.E.R.'s performance at the 2019 Grammys captured the attention of the music world.

**"I practiced my Grammy speech as a child. I've literally imagined that moment over and over again throughout the years, so it's very special to me. Win or not, I just want it to be the exact moment that I imagined."[1]**

**–H.E.R.**

about: a 21-year-old R&B musician who went by the name of H.E.R.

"One of the best surprises of the 2019 Grammy nominations was all the love heaped on H.E.R., the low-profile R&B

H.E.R. arrived at the 2019 Grammys surrounded by anticipation for not just her five nominations but also her performance at the awards show.

artist who earned five nods, including album of the year and best new artist," wrote *USA Today* in the lead-up to the night's festivities. "Clearly, the Grammys voters have a serious affection for Gabi Wilson, who performs as H.E.R., suggesting that she may take home the best-new-artist field."[2]

## RED CARPET JITTERS

Ahead of the big event, musicians and reporters roamed the red carpet outside the Staples Center in Los Angeles, California. Clad in a gorgeous blue and purple sequined outfit and a pair of blue-tinted sunglasses, H.E.R. was nearly overcome with excitement. A pair of reporters stopped to ask how she was feeling about the night.

"Oh my gosh. Twenty years ago, Lauryn Hill won five Grammys, and this year I'm nominated for five, so that's telling to me," H.E.R.

### AN OUTFIT MADE TO SHINE

Awards shows like the Grammys or the Oscars are mostly about celebrating performers' talent. But many fans also insist that part of what makes the ceremonies so thrilling to watch is the outfits. Dressed in a flowing and vibrant jumpsuit, H.E.R. did not disappoint. "H.E.R.'s 2019 Grammys outfit proved she can hang with the big boys," wrote StyleCaster's Maggie Griswold.[3]

told them. "I feel like I'm exactly where I'm supposed to be. I'm just living in the moment."[4]

At the ceremony, she was not only up for awards but would also be performing. H.E.R. had spent a lot of time in rehearsals with her band. She'd had dozens of fittings with her style team to design a glamorous, eye-catching outfit for the occasion. She had also hired the famous musical instrument company Fender Guitars to make her a brand-new guitar to match her clothes. By the time the award show came, she knew she was ready.

"I just have to remember that this was meant for me, this moment," H.E.R. told the reporters. "I can't enjoy it if I'm nervous. I've just gotta enjoy it."[5]

## A ONE-OF-A-KIND STRATOCASTER

A week before the Grammys were set to take place, H.E.R. had a unique request. She needed a guitar that would match her outfit when she performed on that legendary stage for the first time. She called her favorite guitar company, Fender, and asked if it would be possible to make a clear Stratocaster.

Normally such a project would take at least a month. But master builder Scott Buehl at Fender Custom Shop said he would drop everything to make it happen. It wasn't easy. Acrylic is a delicate material that can crack during the manufacturing process. But after a week of labor, it was finished. "It was a great experience," Buehl said. "It's clear as glass and came out looking like a jewel."[6]

H.E.R. thrilled fans at the Grammys and at home with her impressive guitar skills.

## SHREDDING IT

H.E.R.'s confidence paid off. When it came time to perform, she strutted onstage dressed in a shimmering silver pantsuit, strumming her guitar like she owned the room. With a single spotlight on her, she sang a killer version of "Hard Place," an emotional ballad off her extended play (EP) *I Used to Know Her: Part 2.*

As the audience watched in awe, she belted out the first verse, singing about love, heartache, and the frustration that comes with being stuck in a soured relationship. Then, during the guitar solo, an unexpected thing happened. The stage lights brightened like an electric red-and-orange sunset. A full band and choir appeared behind H.E.R. As they joined her on the chorus, she shredded her guitar solo and the crowd went wild.

It was an unforgettable performance. MTV News reporter Madeline Roth summarized what had happened the following day. "Who is H.E.R.? That was a question on many people's minds after the breakout R&B star received a windfall of Grammy nominations in December," Roth wrote. "Her performance at the awards show on Sunday

## H.E.R. 'S FIRST GUITAR

During the 2019 Grammys, reporters and fans alike praised H.E.R. for her guitar solo. The response wasn't surprising. H.E.R. taught herself to play when she was a kid. She watched YouTube videos of Prince and B. B. King and got plenty of help from her musician father. "My dad took me to the Guitar Center and bought me a mini black-and-white Fender Stratocaster," she told reporter Ted Stryker after the Grammys. "He taught me to play the blues."[7]

night, though, answered it definitively: She's a musical force to be reckoned with whose name you're going to remember for a long, long time."[8]

## THE BIG MOMENT

H.E.R. loved the standing ovation she received after her performance. But nothing could have prepared her for what was about to come next. In a field of four other nominees, including Toni Braxton, The Carters, Lalah Hathaway, and PJ Morton, her song with Daniel Caesar, "Best Part," won for Best R&B Performance.

Then, after the award for Best Country Album was presented to Kacey Musgraves for *Golden Hour*, the nominees for Best R&B Album of the Year were announced. H.E.R. was up against some of the same competitors. Toni Braxton, Lalah Hathaway, and PJ Morton were all in the running, along with Leon Bridges. But at the end of it all, H.E.R. took home the trophy for her 2017 self-titled EP, *H.E.R.*

H.E.R. didn't win all of the awards she was nominated for. But she still felt elated by the results. In an interview

following the ceremony, she gushed to reporters who wanted to hear what the rising star had to say. "This means the world to me only because it's confirmation," H.E.R. said. "I sometimes have doubts. . . . Am I doing the right thing? Am I making the right music? This is proof that I'm exactly where I'm supposed to be."[10]

## AN INSPIRATION TO MANY

In 2021 H.E.R. was considered by critics to be one of the most talented young stars coming up in the R&B world. With her long, curly tresses and signature sunglasses, she is known not just for her soulful ballads and undeniable talent on the guitar, but also for her fashion sense and demonstrated confidence onstage.

### NOTABLE MOMENTS FROM THE 2019 GRAMMYS

Fans tune in to the Grammys to find out whether their favorite artists will win the night's top awards. They also look out for other notable moments that make the actual ceremony more interesting. In 2019 there were plenty. Legend Diana Ross wished herself a happy 75th birthday. Alicia Keys performed a medley on not one but two pianos. She also brought out friends Lady Gaga, Jada Pinkett Smith, Jennifer Lopez, and former First Lady Michelle Obama to talk about the impact music had on their lives.

H.E.R.'s unconventional career path has taken her on a winding journey from obscurity to stardom.

"She's a multi-instrumentalist performing contemporary rhythm and blues in the truest sense," wrote *Los Angeles Times* journalist Gerrick D. Kennedy in 2018. "[She] stayed true to her core and pierced the bass rattling sounds of rap with several EPs bursting with brooding, slow dripping soul anchored by a velvety, rich voice that announced H.E.R. as one of the most exciting R&B talents in recent years."[11]

But H.E.R.'s path to stardom wasn't like that of many aspiring young musicians. She wasn't discovered on social media like Halsey or Shawn Mendes. She didn't nail a record contract after competing on *American Idol* like Kelly Clarkson or Madison Vandenburg. She followed her own unique route to fame. It all began when she was a young girl growing up in California.

# CHILD PRODIGY

**A** lot of kids like to sing in the shower or hum to themselves on the way to school. But for Gabriella "Gabi" Wilson, singing wasn't just a hobby. It was a calling.

When she was four years old, Gabi recorded a rendition of "London Bridge Is Falling Down" on tape. She took the lead and her aunts accompanied her on backup vocals. Instead of just singing the lyrics, she made the nursery rhyme into a full song. According to Gabi's family, it was a turning point that foreshadowed her career as a musician. "That was the very beginning, when they recognized that I loved [singing]," Gabi later explained in an interview. "There was something in me that was calling me toward music."[1]

## SURROUNDED BY MUSIC

Gabi Wilson was born on June 27, 1997. She grew up in Vallejo, a city located in California's San Francisco Bay Area. From the time she was little, Gabi was surrounded by family and music. She lived with her parents and maternal

**The roots of Gabi Wilson's musical career go all the way back to her childhood.**

**Performances of nursery rhymes on tape were some of Gabi's earliest recordings.**

grandparents, who were Filipino. On nights when Agnes, Gabi's mother, was making dinner, she and Gabi would belt out songs by Earth, Wind & Fire; Sly and the Family Stone; and the Queen of Soul, Aretha Franklin.

Gabi also spent much of her childhood watching her Black father, Kenny, and his friends play jam sessions in the living room. Kenny was in an R&B band called the Urban Bushmen and often rehearsed with the group late into the night. When Gabi was old enough to hold a mic, her dad let her join in during practice. He taught her to play Prince's "Purple Rain." Before long, she had learned to play the piano, drums, guitar, and bass.

## IT'S SHOWTIME

Gabi adored singing and playing music with her parents. But she wasn't content to just jam out at home. Even at a young age, she longed to perform in front of crowds. When she turned six, Kenny started booking private gigs for her around town. At eight, she was named California's Most Talented Kid at the state fair. She beat 60 other kids 16 and under for the honor. By nine, she was opening for bands like Tony! Toni! Toné!, Keyshia Cole, and

### A MIXED-RACE BACKGROUND

Gabi Wilson has always embraced her mixed-race heritage. Her Filipino grandparents were an important presence in her household and taught her to respect her ancestors and their culture. Through music and food, her dad's side inspired her to be proud of her African American roots too. "My dad would throw down with the soul food when we had our Black side over," she said in an interview. "Black culture, to me, is so important and I identify with young Black women. I represent young Black women, and I'm proud of that."[2]

The Ohio Players at local concerts. By this time she was writing her own songs.

On July 28, 2007, Kenny took the then ten-year-old to Oakland, a neighboring city. Gabi hoped to audition for *Showtime at the Apollo*, a famous variety television show in New York City that featured live performances from new musicians and comedians. Though she was turned away initially, fate was on her side. The event coordinators for the Apollo Theater saw her promotional tape and changed their minds. After listening to her sing, they decided she was ready to take on the Big Apple.

On September 23, 2007, she stepped onstage at the Apollo Theater. As the

## THE URBAN BUSHMEN BAND

Founded by Gabi's father, Kenny, the Urban Bushmen describe themselves as a classic R&B, blues, and neo soul band based in Northern California. The band consists of Kenny Wilson and Odys Burns on lead guitar, Christian Houston on keyboard, Alton McGriff on bass, Greg McGriff on drums, Brian "Lakeside" Lake on percussion, Jimmie Weaver on saxophone, Cecil Kirkpatrick on trumpet, and Mike Brooks on trombone. Karl Bracy handles lead vocals while the rest of the band sings backup. "We were all friends ten to 15 years before we were a band," said Houston about the Bushmen. "We're pretty humble cats and it's nice to be in a band where people's egos aren't so inflated that they can't get their heads in the door."[3]

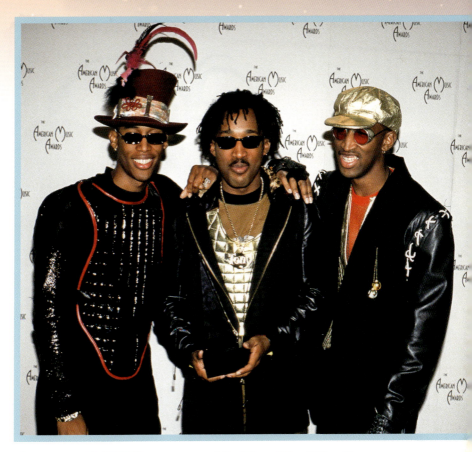

The young Gabi Wilson opened for Tony! Toni! Toné!, an influential three-person R&B group that was most popular in the late 1980s and mid-1990s.

lights went up, she belted out "Freeway of Love," a 1973

hit by Aretha Franklin. The audience was amazed that

such a stunning voice could come out of such a small kid.

Her parents were proud too. "I just hope her fan base

can grow and that it leads to her doing bigger and better

## APOLLO SEND-OFF

The Wilsons were thrilled that Gabi would be performing at the Apollo Theater in New York City. But the trip for three would be expensive. To help raise money for the journey, Gabi's family threw a fundraiser. On September 7, 2007, they staged a musical event at the Fetterly Playhouse for the Arts in Vallejo. Gabi and her father performed alongside saxophonist and dancer Andrew Beal and *American Idol* vocalists Donnie Williams and Olivia Jasmine. "We're just so happy a lot of people are trying to support her," Agnes Wilson said.[5]

"[Gabi Wilson] is outrageously talented. She has the heart for it and has an amazing voice. And she's passionate about the music at such a young age."[6]
—*Musician and dancer Andrew Beal*

things," Kenny said at the time. "It's a stepping stone to the next level."[4]

## PLAYING THE MEDIA CIRCUIT

After the show at the Apollo, it seemed everyone wanted to hear Gabi sing and play music. She was booked on a number of high-profile morning and evening talk shows, including *The Maury Povich Show* on his "Most Talented Kids" segment. To finish the year, Gabi performed twice on *The Today Show*. The first appearance aired on December 4 during one of President George W. Bush's presidential addresses. Though she played piano and sang

The Apollo Theater is a legendary venue located in Harlem, New York City.

her idol Alicia Keys's "If I Ain't Got You" beautifully, many viewers missed it because they were watching the president instead.

On December 19, *Today* requested that Gabi come back and sing again. As expected, Patti LaBelle, known as the Godmother of Soul, wowed the live audience that day. But Gabi also gave a captivating performance. She sang Keys's single "No One" and captured the hearts of viewers nationwide. "I feel like I'm just in the living room, that's why I'm never nervous," Gabi said in an interview with the hosts during the show.[7]

At the time of her knockout *Today* premiere, Gabi was a fifth grader at North Hills Christian School. She did well in school and earned straight As. When she wasn't practicing music, she loved to write. She had even published a book when she was

## A STAR-SPANGLED PERFORMANCE

Singing the national anthem at a sports game is a great honor for many artists and musicians. On December 15, 2007, that honor fell to Gabi Wilson. She was chosen to perform "The Star-Spangled Banner" at a Los Angeles Lakers basketball game against the Golden State Warriors. She wore a Warriors number 5 jersey, later autographed by point guard Baron Davis. During the game's halftime show, she performed "Boogie Oogie Oogie" by Taste of Honey and Prince's "How Come You Don't Call Me." The crowd gave her a standing ovation. "Everyone loved it," Kenny Wilson said. "The cool thing was that on the way to the dressing room, Kobe [Bryant] came by and shook her hand and said, 'Great job.'"[8]

Singing songs by one of her musical inspirations, Alicia Keys, helped Gabi raise her profile as a young artist.

eight called *Anything on Earth Poems*. But in spite of those other interests, it had already become clear that her future would be in show business.

"[My friends] are really proud of me. They support me a lot and go to my concerts. I really appreciate them. And I still get to hang out with them. We have sleepovers, or we go to the mall or we go shopping."[9]

—*Gabi Wilson, 2007*

# AMERICA'S "NEXT BIG THING"

**D**uring the first few years after Gabi turned ten, she was busier than ever. From singing the national anthem at sports games to booking gigs on *Good Morning America* and *The View*, the talented young star was frequently on the road. Motivated and confident, she loved getting up in front of audiences large and small to perform. With continued support from her parents, she was always looking for what would take her career to the next level.

The moment arrived on the day before her twelfth birthday. On June 26, 2009, Gabi performed at the 22nd Annual Rhythm & Soul Music Awards. The event was hosted by the American Society of Composers, Authors and Publishers (ASCAP) and held in Beverly Hills, California. The ceremony gave out awards for the top songs on the

A performance in the summer of 2009 helped take Gabi's young career in new directions.

In her Rhythm & Soul Music Awards performance, Gabi showed her skills on the bass.

## NOT YOUR TYPICAL SCHOOL GYRL

Gabi Wilson had a busy adolescence. In addition to playing four instruments, singing, and writing, Gabi also tried her hand at acting. She landed a minor role in a made-for-TV movie on Nickelodeon directed by Nick Cannon. It was called *School Gyrls* and featured three freshmen at an all-girls boarding school who loved to sing and dance. Gabi played herself. She was just wrapping up shooting when the Rhythm & Soul Music Awards aired.

2008 R&B/Hip-Hop, Rap, and Gospel *Billboard* charts. It was attended by more than 650 songwriters, recording artists, and music industry notables.

As part of a tribute to Alicia Keys, who received the ASCAP's Golden Note Award that evening, Gabi played a version of the superstar's "If I Ain't Got You" on piano. Then she grabbed her bass, joined the house band, and sang vocals on Keys's "Unbreakable." The audience erupted in a standing ovation. Then Keys grabbed the mic and said, "Give her another round of applause. Miss Gabi Wilson. She's amazing."[1]

**Gabi played piano and sang during the ASCAP awards show.**

## COMPETITION TIME

Not long after Gabi's crowd-pleasing performance at the Rhythm & Soul Music Awards, her fledgling career took another exciting turn. Top executives at Walt Disney Studios had heard the buzz about her and asked her to audition. They were looking for fresh talent for their company and thought Gabi might fit the bill.

Gabi was happy to show them what she could do. She sang two songs, one by Beyoncé and the other by Leona Lewis. The executives were so impressed they introduced her to the producers of the Radio Disney show *Next Big Thing*. After the producers listened to a recording of a song she wrote called "My Music,"

### "MY MUSIC": A FAMILY EFFORT

Like many things in her life, Gabi's first song was a success in part because of the love, support, and help she received from her family. It came to be after an afternoon of watching concerts on YouTube with her dad. He showed her videos by Sly and the Family Stone. She showed him some from Hannah Montana. They debated about which music was better. Within a few hours, Gabi had come up with the bass line for her first song. Then she wrote the lyrics. The day before her meeting with Disney, she recorded a demo of "My Music" in a Hollywood studio. Her dad said it had the sound of a hit.

she was hired for the show
on the spot.

On September 23, 2009,
Radio Disney launched
its second season of *Next
Big Thing* (*NBT*). Over the
course of ten weeks, five
up-and-coming unsigned

"It would be great to be the *Next Big Thing* because I've always wanted to do big things. . . . [It] would complete everything I've always dreamed of."[2]

—*Gabi Wilson*

**Exposure on Radio Disney represented a major opportunity for Gabi to reach new listeners.**

artists—all around Gabi's age—competed for the top prize. In addition to Gabi, there was Josh Golden, Kropp Circle, Jasmine Sagginario, and Cymphonique. The rules were pretty straightforward. *NBT* fans would first listen to performances from all of the artists on Radio Disney. Then they would vote for their favorite act overall. The highest-ranked *NBT* artist would have the opportunity to have a single featured on the upcoming release *Radio Disney Jams 12*.

The competition was fierce. Gabi was the first musician to be featured. "My Music" was played on the Radio Disney playlist for two weeks. Viewers were also treated to a short video of Gabi talking about what her life was like behind the scenes. When the final voting period began on December 2, thousands of kids weighed in.

The winner of *Next Big Thing* was announced on December 11. Gabi didn't win—Jasmine Sagginario captured that honor. Still, because of the competition, millions of teens across the country were now aware of who Gabi Wilson was. Better yet, they wanted to hear more from her.

## A RECORD CONTRACT

By the time Gabi turned 13, she was playing music more than ever, booking gigs, and practicing for hours every day. On June 27, 2010, her birthday, she performed at the BET Awards at the Shrine Auditorium in Los Angeles. Introduced by Queen Latifah, she sang a gorgeous a cappella rendition of verses from Alicia Keys's "Fallin'."

When she was 16, she got her driver's permit, as many teens do at this age. But unlike her peers, she also added many new celebrity-level accomplishments to her resume. She became an ambassador for Kuboo, an app that allows kids to learn and interact with their friends online in a virtual reality world. She appeared in a reality show produced by actor

### CHARITABLE PLAYING

In 2013 and 2014, Gabi's schedule was even more packed than usual. In addition to her schoolwork as a high school junior and long hours in the recording studio, she also found time to play charity benefits for important causes. She performed at the Hard Rock Cafe in New York City to raise money for St. Mary's Healthcare System for Children, a hospital that treats kids and teens with long-term health needs. She also sang "What Is Hip?" with members of the band Tower of Power in Fairfield, Connecticut, to raise money for cancer research.

**Singer, rapper, and actor Queen Latifah appeared onstage with Gabi at the BET Awards in 2010.**

and rapper Nick Cannon's Ncredible Entertainment. She was invited to play for Alicia Keys in the Grammy winner's studio. She also performed on a revived version of the

**Gabi secured a record contract in 2014, seemingly setting her up to launch her recording career.**

variety show *Soul Train*, hosted by Cannon. Yet despite these wins, Gabi had her mind set on her ultimate dream: a record deal. "Vocally, I really improved [this past year]. I feel like I've accomplished a lot. I'm really close to getting what I want," she said in an interview at the time.[3]

Before long, that hope became a reality. In 2014, Gabi signed a contract with RCA Records/Sony Entertainment. With more than 60 original songs under her belt, she went into a recording studio in New York to lay down some tracks. She familiarized herself with professional audio equipment. She also learned the business side of the music industry with the help of her dad and Jeff Robinson, founder of MBK Entertainment, Gabi's management company.

When she was done, Gabi released a debut single titled "Something to Prove" under her own name. She was chosen as the Music Matters Artist at the 2014 BET Awards and performed the song there. But aside from that, there was little fanfare. Gabi was disappointed by the lack of recognition, but she continued to record more songs in the studio. "[Avoiding the pitfalls of the

"[Gabi is] an absolute all-around and most talented young artist. I look forward to helping her build a legendary career. Gabi isn't just talented, she is the next superstar on the rise."[4]
*—Jeff Robinson, MBK Entertainment*

## TWO YOUNG ARTISTS

Ever since she was old enough to hold a guitar, Gabi idolized Alicia Keys. Keys respected Gabi's determination and will to succeed. The two artists also had a lot in common, especially their origin stories. "I was signed when I was 14 and then had been developing all the way up to the first album and probably a lot like [her]," Keys told NBC. "You have your dreams and you have your wishes and of course you find yourself hoping that it's going to all work out. Sometimes you've got to sit for a minute and wait for that right moment. That's hard—that discipline is almost just as hard."[5]

music industry] is a lot harder than people think," Gabi told Cannon in an interview. "But at the end of the day, it's about me working at my craft and getting better at what I do."[6]

At the end of 2014, something happened that no one in the music industry or Gabi's growing fan base expected. She vanished not only from the spotlight but from the public eye altogether. As far as the music world was concerned, the rising superstar Gabi Wilson had simply ceased to exist.

# WHO IS H.E.R.?

For two years, Gabi Wilson appeared to be living under the radar. The young musician with the musicianship of Prince and a voice that had been compared to that of superstars like Beyoncé and Aretha Franklin stayed largely out of the public eye. Though she had signed with a record label, she didn't put out an album. The details of her life at this time are not publicly known. At the time, it appeared as though Gabi had stopped releasing music altogether—or at least that she had stopped trying to become the next Alicia Keys.

The R&B world turned its attention elsewhere. Then, in September 2016, a new musician appeared on the scene. Her music was starting to make waves on the radio and on social media. But who was she?

## A MYSTERIOUS NEW ARTIST

On September 9, 2016, an anonymous singer who went by the name H.E.R. (which stands for "Having Everything Revealed") released her debut EP, *H.E.R., Vol. 1*. The cover

Gabi Wilson's return to the music world under the name H.E.R. was deliberately mysterious.

featured a dark silhouette of the back of a curly-haired woman surrounded by a vibrant blue background. In advance of the album's release, RCA Records sent out a press release to the media with an early stream of the album. "I can't tell you much about H.E.R. just yet," the press release said. "But give it a listen and let me know what you think."[1]

The EP's packaging didn't include any biographical information about H.E.R., and it didn't include any liner notes providing detailed information about the making of the album. It just outlined the tracks and listed credits for the songwriters, musicians, and producer. But the seven songs spoke for themselves. Many, including "Losing" and "Focus," were about a universal topic: learning how to

## SOCIAL MEDIA AFLAME

In September 2016, R&B fans got wind of a new artist whose music was appearing on the airwaves and trending on YouTube. Word got around especially quickly because Alicia Keys posted a tweet that read, "Have you heard @HERMusicx yet?" She included a link to some songs. Judging by the responses, some of Keys's fans thought she was releasing a new album. But most others took it as a sign to check out this artist's tracks. "Track 5 on Repeat. #Focus. Thanks for enlightening us AliciA," wrote one follower.[2]

be strong before, during, and after a breakup. "[I wanted people to] feel they could relate to [the music] without having to look at me," H.E.R. later told *Billboard*. "I just [wanted] them to realize that I'm like them."[3]

As soon as the EP was released, big-name celebrities in the R&B, hip-hop, and soul world took notice. It earned praise from other RCA artists, including Alicia Keys and Bryson Tiller. More musicians, such as Wyclef Jean and Pusha T, spoke out about the album, and it slowly gained buzz. Rihanna even uploaded a clip onto Instagram with "Focus" playing in the background. The video went viral, receiving five million hits.

## "CLOAKED ARTISTS ARE ANNOYING, BUT . . ."

In an article written following the release of *H.E.R., Vol. 1*, music reporter Stacy-Ann Ellis wrote something that was on a lot of people's minds at the time: "I have a known disdain for artists that obsess over hiding. Living their lives behind cloaks while their voices hover in the foreground," she wrote. "Faux mystique, I like to call it. Or annoying."[4]

But by the end of the piece, she had come clean about her true feelings about this specific artist's decision to remain anonymous. In short, Ellis believed it was a win-win. "Her anonymity takes away the what's, where's and who's. What she looks like. Where she's from. Who she could be singing about and the context for her woes," Ellis wrote. "She simply presents them as is, leaving your mind and your experiences to do the handiwork."[5]

In just a few weeks' time, *H.E.R., Vol. 1* went on to reach Number 12 on *Billboard*'s Top R&B Albums chart and Number 28 on *Billboard*'s Top R&B/Hip-Hop Albums chart. It peaked at Number 1 on the iTunes R&B/Soul Albums chart.

"As a young woman, I experienced high school and heartbreak, and the music I started to write was a little bit more poetic. . . . The real raw emotional things that sit in the back of our minds, that you were afraid to say? That's how I started to write my music. And that's how *H.E.R., Vol. 1* came about."[6]

—*H.E.R.*

Mentions by other artists, including Rihanna, helped build awareness of H.E.R.'s music.

But on the day of the EP's release, no one actually knew who the artist was—and the artist herself wasn't saying a word.

## CLUES REVEALED

Despite the mystery surrounding *H.E.R., Vol. 1*, the public's confusion about the true identity of H.E.R. proved to be fairly short-lived. The day after the EP's release, music reporter Lauren Nostro published an article titled "Here's the Secret Identity of H.E.R., the Mysterious Singer Signed to RCA Records."[7] In it, she wrote about H.E.R.'s cover of Drake's "Jungle" on *Vol. 1* and insisted that the song "gives it all away." The article also included two links to "Jungle" on Soundcloud—one from *H.E.R., Vol. 1* and the other

### A LOW-KEY RELEASE

When most musicians put out an album, they do so with much fanfare and advance publicity. In 2016, the same year H.E.R.'s debut EP was released, for example, Rihanna produced her eighth studio album, *ANTI*. To get the word out, she signed a $25 million contract with Samsung to promote its products in exchange for sponsoring her seventh worldwide tour. But H.E.R. didn't do any major press interviews. She also didn't create any official press photos. Instead, she let the music speak for itself.

## INSPIRED BY DRAKE

Just a few months after she released her first single, "Something to Prove," Gabi Wilson went back into the studio to lay down more tracks. In between recording more original songs, she also worked on a version of Drake's "Jungle" and added her own personal spin. When it was finished, she released it on the music site Complex. "['Jungle'] is my favorite song off of Drake's new mixtape. What I got from it is touching on something I'm dealing with at the moment," she said in the accompanying interview. "I'm inspired by the creative minds I surround myself with, the places I've seen, and the situations I've been in. When I'm emotional and I hear the right melodies and chords in my head, the right words come out."[10]

from Gabi Wilson. "From a quick listen, it's not hard to tell they're the same artist," Nostro wrote.[8]

Following that article, speculative posts on Twitter, Facebook, and Instagram by curious and adoring fans popped up all over the internet. National media outlets picked up the trail, publishing follow-up pieces about the similarities between H.E.R. and Gabi Wilson and praising the album in general. National Public Radio listed *H.E.R., Vol. 1* as one of "5 essential R&B albums you slept on" in 2016. *Forbes* included H.E.R. in its list of "5 Alternative R&B Artists to Look Out for in 2017." By January 2017, four months after its release, the album had racked up 30 million streams.[9]

But even with all the positive publicity, RCA Records declined to confirm whether Nostro's reporting about the link between H.E.R. and Gabi Wilson was accurate. So did H.E.R.'s manager, Jeff Robinson. In the fall of 2016, many fans and music reporters alike were left wondering why H.E.R. was maintaining such an air of mystery about her identity.

*Vol. 1* is a seven-track project featuring a young woman deep in the feels. Her formula is straightforward but shouldn't be underestimated. She's taking what's old and making a whole new pot of gumbo."[11]

—*Bobby Carter, NPR*

# THE RISE TO FAME

For months following the release of *H.E.R., Vol. 1*, fans and music media alike were all but convinced that H.E.R. and Gabi Wilson were the same person. They scoured social media to hunt down clues that would confirm their suspicions. Despite the fact that H.E.R. and Wilson had different Twitter and Instagram accounts, H.E.R.'s followers insisted the two artists were identical. *Forbes* entertainment reporter Natalie Robehmed even went so far as to check the songs from *Vol. 1* on ASCAP's service that allows users to look up songwriting credits by artist. When she looked for Gabriella Wilson, her search came up with 20 tracks. All listed H.E.R. as the performer.

With more and more articles being published about the link between H.E.R. and Wilson, H.E.R. began to loosen up about the connection. She shared details about her artistic process in interviews and gave details

H.E.R. used her new identity to give her career a fresh start.

about her music-heavy childhood that clearly lined up with Wilson's. Instead of avoiding the topic altogether, she also began to answer reporters' questions about the evasive *Vol. 1* album cover. "You have easy access to what everybody's doing 24/7 and [the mystery] was kinda my way of getting away from that," she told *Billboard*.[1]

H.E.R. did her best to shift the focus away from whether she was Gabi Wilson. In an industry in which female singers are often judged not by the quality of their music but by their sex appeal, she also tried to avoid discussing her looks or why she often wore sunglasses in photos. Instead, she zeroed in on what she thought was most significant: her music and its effect on her audience. "I did exactly what I wanted to do. . . . People are coming to my shows not to see what I look like but to connect with my music," she later told the *Los Angeles Times*. "Young women, especially Black women, are faced with so many pressures in this industry. And we give in to what we're supposed to look like or what we're supposed to be like. I didn't want any of that."[2]

## BUILDING BUZZ

After years of staying in the shadows, H.E.R. felt ready to take her career to the next level, especially after the success of her first EP. On June 16, 2017, she released a second EP, entitled *H.E.R., Vol. 2*. Designed similarly to the first, the album features a dark silhouette on the cover against a warm orange background. It contains eight tracks, all ballads and slow jams about love, sex, relationships, and identity. In sultry songs

### SIGNATURE SUNGLASSES

Throughout her career, H.E.R. has always been intentional about her wardrobe decisions. In the beginning, she wore a lot of stylish but comfortable clothing, such as baggy sweatshirts and leggings. She never appeared in videos or onstage without a pair of sunglasses. "I have phases where I wear one pair of shades," she said in 2017. "I found these, they're goggles, at Nordstrom Rack. I love Ray-Bans, but I don't want to exclude any brand. . . . Gucci has really dope glasses."[3]

> "When I think about the reason why I dropped the projects under the name H.E.R., the people resonate with it so much because H.E.R. is everyone. All my stories have no face attached to it, there's no name attached to it, so it's like you have no choice but to be attached to the feeling and the emotion and relating it to your personal diary."[5]
>
> —H.E.R.

such as "Every Kind of Way" and "Say It Again," H.E.R. describes owning her sexuality and giving in to passion. In "I Won't," she croons about finding the courage to say no to a lover she isn't interested in. On "Still Down," she addresses both romantic insecurities and competition for a partner.

Like its predecessor, *Vol. 2* was well-received by the press. "[H.E.R.] achieves all the ambiance of grown-and-sexy throwback R&B and modernizes it with the help of her mainstay producer DJ Camper," wrote Briana Younger for Pitchfork. "At her most melancholic, she sounds like a person who still loves love—naive, perhaps, but always willing to give it a chance."[4] The EP peaked at Number 49 on the all-genre *Billboard* 200 chart and Number 22 on the Top R&B/Hip-Hop Albums chart.

To promote *Vol. 2*, H.E.R. joined musicians Bryson Tiller, Khalid, and others for the BET Experience concert

H.E.R.'s performances in 2017 showcased the development of the instrumental and singing skills she had been working on since childhood.

at the Staples Center in Los Angeles on June 23, 2017. She also joined Tiller on his Set It Off tour. It kicked off on August 3 in Atlanta, Georgia. From there and over the course of 27 scheduled shows, the musicians played concerts in many locations, including

"It seems that the mysterious songstress aims at warmer territory for [*H.E.R., Vol. 2*], offering a welcome introduction to her more sensual side in the process."[6]

—*D-Money, soul music website SoulBounce*

## THE BET EXPERIENCE CONCERT

On June 23, 2017, an event many R&B fans had been waiting for finally took place. The enigmatic artist H.E.R. was scheduled to appear live and in person. As the stage rotated to start the show, a fan was heard squealing, "I've waited so long for this."[8]

H.E.R. performed with her back to the audience. She opened with "Say It Again" from *Vol. 2*. Then she sang "Wait for It," which flowed into Floetry's "Say Yes." Other covers included Rihanna's "Yeah I Said It" and Kendrick Lamar's "Love." *Billboard*'s Ashley Lyle wrote, "Finishing off the set in a subtle way singing as the stage rotated out, the audience was left with an introduction of one of R&B's most promising acts."[9]

New Orleans, Louisiana; Las Vegas, Nevada; Philadelphia, Pennsylvania; and New York City. The whirlwind tour wrapped up in Louisville, Kentucky, on September 16.

## ON THE ROAD AGAIN

By the fall of 2017, H.E.R. was exhausted from all the traveling. At that point, *Vol. 1* and *Vol. 2* combined had racked up more than 213 million streams worldwide across all digital platforms.[7] But instead of taking a breather, she built on the momentum. On October 13, she released the official music video for "Every Kind of Way," a track from *Vol. 2*. In addition, she put out "2," a song from *Vol. 2: The B Sides*, a new release that was made available for download on October 20. That same day, RCA released a deluxe digital edition of *Vol. 1* and *Vol. 2*. It contained all the songs from the EPs, plus six additional songs. These included "2" and a duet with musician Daniel Caesar called "Best Part."

To promote these new releases, H.E.R. embarked on the Lights On tour, the first headlining tour of her career. Beginning on November 5 in Washington, DC, she performed on college campuses and at major venues in

**American singer and rapper Bryson Tiller played on tour with H.E.R. in the summer of 2017.**

**H.E.R. quickly built up a large fan base that was excited to see her perform live.**

more than a dozen cities across the United States and

Canada, including Chicago, Illinois; Toronto, Ontario; New

York City; San Francisco, California; Detroit, Michigan; and

Vancouver, British Columbia. When the tickets went on sale, they sold out for all of the dates in ten minutes.

Thanks in part to the tour and H.E.R.'s rising popularity, the deluxe package of *Vol. 1* and *Vol. 2* was a huge success. The release was named one of the top ten albums of the year by the Associated Press. It reached Number 23 on the *Billboard* 200 chart and Number 14 on *Billboard*'s Top R&B/Hip-Hop Albums chart. On Spotify, H.E.R. had 2.5 million monthly listeners. Users of the service had streamed the songs "Best Part" and "Losing" more than 18 million times each.[10] H.E.R. was riding on a wave of popularity that didn't seem to be ebbing anytime soon.

## THE MAKING OF "BEST PART"

By the end of 2017, one of H.E.R.'s most popular songs was a collaboration with Daniel Caesar called "Best Part." It wasn't originally planned as a cooperative effort. She was in the recording studio working on some new tracks. Tunji, a friend from RCA Records, stopped by and introduced H.E.R. to his friend Caesar. H.E.R. and Caesar started jamming, and before long a duet emerged. "We didn't plan on having a session. We just started playing music for each other and talking," H.E.R. recalled. "He had his guitar, and I had my guitar, so we started playing. The song came out organically, just bouncing melodies back and forth."[11]

# H.E.R.'S FIRST WIN

In early 2018, 20-year-old H.E.R. was living out of a suitcase in Brooklyn, New York. She was working on songs for a new album and juggling a calendar of concerts. As usual, her schedule was jam-packed with music-related firsts.

In March, H.E.R. hit a milestone when she took the Lights On tour overseas. She embarked on a ten-city trip, stopping to play in venues across Europe, including London, England; Paris, France; Cologne, Munich, and Frankfurt, Germany; and Amsterdam in the Netherlands. Many of the concerts sold out quickly. Some celebrities even showed up, such as Janet Jackson, who posted photos on Instagram of hanging out backstage with H.E.R. in London.

On June 24, H.E.R. was up for Best Female R&B/Pop Artist and Best New Artist at the BET Awards. She was

H.E.R.'s career moves in 2018 would earn her critical acclaim and many new fans around the world.

61

## H.E.R. LIGHTS UP PARIS

On March 12, 2018, H.E.R. stopped in Paris to headline a concert as part of the Lights On tour. The venue was cloaked in hazy red, green, and blue light, and fans were packed inside to see their favorite new R&B star perform. Decked out in a pair of gray camo Champion overalls, high-heeled platform boots, and a pair of white sunglasses, H.E.R. nailed her hour-long set. She played a number of songs from *Vol. 1* and *Vol. 2*, including "Focus," "Avenue," "Still Down," "Every Kind of Way," and "Best Part." Her French fans loved the show—especially after she invited some lucky people in the front onstage to dance.

"You are a sweet and talented soul. Congratulations on your first sold out show in London! I couldn't help but sing along with you, I knew every single word. I'm excited for your journey, never change who you are."[1]
–Janet Jackson in an Instagram post

also invited to perform. Clad in a gorgeous aqua dress with cinched-up sides and pleather leggings, platform sneakers, glittery jewelry, and her signature shades, she sang a moving rendition of "Focus" in a shroud of fog and smoke. Then she grabbed her matching aqua electric guitar and shredded her solo as the crowd went wild. "Focus" then flowed into "Best Part" as Daniel Caesar stepped onstage, followed by a cover of Lauryn Hill and D'Angelo's "Nothing Even Matters."

H.E.R. didn't win any awards that night. Beyoncé took home Best Female R&B/Pop Artist and SZA won Best New Artist. But

**H.E.R. performed with Canadian singer-songwriter Daniel Caesar at the 2018 BET Awards.**

the YouTube video of H.E.R.'s performance immediately went viral, with fans raving about her voice and musical talent and comparing her to Jimi Hendrix and Prince. "It was crazy," H.E.R. told *Billboard*. "Live, I knew I was going to really be able to showcase my musicality. . . . It was a shocking thing for people."[2]

## I USED TO KNOW HER

Hot on the heels of her BET performance, H.E.R. joined Chris Brown for portions of his *Heartbreak on a Full Moon* tour. She signed on as one of the opening acts, along with 6LACK and Rich the Kid. The 27-stop tour began in Seattle, Washington, in June and stretched into August, finishing in Las Vegas, Nevada.

At the conclusion of her portion of the tour, and without a moment's rest, H.E.R. released another EP on August 3 in advance of her first full-length compilation. Titled *I Used to Know Her: The Prelude*, the EP has six tracks, including "Lost Souls" (featuring DJ Scratch), "Could've Been"

### JOKESTER ON THE ROAD

Life as a touring musician can be grueling. With a jam-packed schedule of concerts over a short period of time, thousands of miles covered, and plenty of sleepless nights spent crammed into a crowded tour bus, it's typical for musicians to get very little rest. But H.E.R. found a way to have fun with it. On July 27, 2018, she posted a YouTube video showing what the experience was like for her. In it, she walked the viewer throughout the bus, highlighting the sights. Then, out of nowhere, she took a can of shaving cream and sprayed one of her fellow musicians in the face.

(featuring Bryson Tiller), and "As I Am." The songs explore common topics for H.E.R., including romance, flirting, and sex. But they also delve deeper into the mental and emotional changes H.E.R. was experiencing as she transitioned into adulthood. "This prelude is definitely extremely emotional, but it's more pieces to the puzzle of my perspective that I've created up until now," she said in an interview. "I'm 21 years old, and I've experienced a lot of things being on the road . . . meeting other people, relationships, whatever it is. *I Used to Know Her* is my perspective and where I am currently at in the things I've been thinking about and going through."[3]

## THE BEST (OR WORST) LIFE MUSIC FESTIVAL

In the fall of 2018, music fans were gearing up for an exciting new event. Set for September 15 at the RC Cola Plant in Miami, Florida, the inaugural Best Life Music Festival was expected to attract 8,000 people. Some of the acts scheduled to perform included Ella Mai, Xavier Omär, Snoh Aalegra, R.LUM.R, Arin Ray, Ari Chi, SaintLee, and Nohemy. But what many festivalgoers were looking forward to the most was the headliner: H.E.R.

Unfortunately, the concert ended up being a disaster. For one, it started three hours late. The schedule got mixed up, leaving some acts unable to perform while others were forced to cut their sets in half. Worst of all, it was hot and the vendors ran out of water. Still, when H.E.R. took the stage around midnight, the audience ate up her hour-long set. "H.E.R's powerful set almost made the long day worth it," *Miami New Times* reporter Cristina Jerome said.[4]

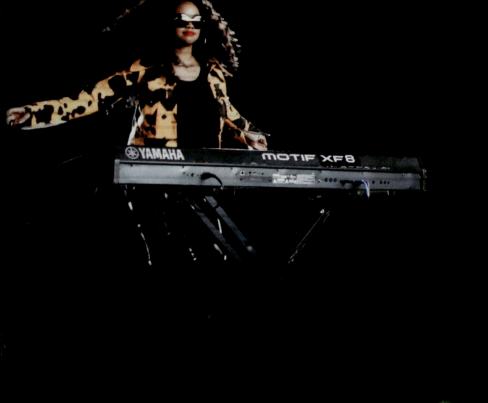

*The Prelude* was an immediate hit. It peaked at Number 1 on *Billboard*'s Top R&B Albums chart. National Public Radio said the EP's tracks "resonate with millennial angst while being sonically evocative of the R&B greats like Sade, Kelly Rowland, Anita Baker and Toni Braxton."[5]

By this time, H.E.R.'s songs had reached one billion combined streams.[6]

Then, on November 2, H.E.R. released the EP *I Used to Know Her: Part 2*. It contained eight songs, including "Carried Away," "I'm Not Going," and "Hard Place."

> "The title *I Used to Know Her* is really just me getting back to my younger self. I was young and fearless when I started music. It came naturally to me, and it was something I loved to do, but I had no insecurities. . . . It's about keeping that fun, that youthful mentality of 'What do I have to lose?'"[8]
>
> *—H.E.R.*

To support the back-to-back EPs, she took off on her second headlining tour, which featured 21 stops around the United States and overseas. With Bri Steves and Tone Stith signed on as openers, the tour kicked off on November 10 in Atlanta, Georgia, and made stops in New York, Chicago, Las Vegas, and other cities. On December 20, H.E.R. closed out the journey in San Francisco.

## BIG NEWS

For H.E.R., 2018 was certainly a banner year. Some of her biggest accomplishments happened toward the end, around the time of her autumn tour. On October 9, she made her *Tonight Show with Jimmy Fallon* debut. In front of a live audience and 2.6 million at-home viewers, she performed a sweeping rendition of "As I Am."[7]

That fall she landed a whopping seven 2018 Soul Train Music Awards nominations—the most of any artist that year, including powerhouse performers Bruno Mars and Cardi B. Some of the most prestigious ones included Best R&B Soul Female Artist, Song of the Year for "Every Kind of Way," the Ashford and Simpson Songwriters Award for "Focus," and Video of the Year for "Avenue." Though H.E.R. didn't win as many awards as she'd hoped, she did pick up two trophies at the November 17 ceremony. She won one for Best Collaboration Performance ("Best Part") and another for Best Album/Mix-Tape (*H.E.R.*).

But the icing on the cake came on the morning of December 7, when the nominations for the 61st Grammy Awards were announced. H.E.R. was nominated for a jaw-dropping five awards: Best Album (*H.E.R.*), Best New Artist, Best R&B Performance ("Best Part"),

## MORE MEMORABLE FIRSTS

For H.E.R., 2018 was a big year for firsts. She completed her first international headlining tour. *I Used to Know Her: The Prelude* reached Number 1 on *Billboard*'s Top R&B Albums chart. Two of her songs also shattered her previous sales records. On October 17, her single "Focus" was certified gold by the Recording Industry Association of America (RIAA), with more than 500,000 units sold.[9] Then, on November 29, "Best Part" was certified platinum, with more than one million units sold.[10]

Best R&B Album (*H.E.R.*), and Best R&B Song ("Focus"). When she heard the news, she posted a video of herself dancing on Instagram. The caption read, in all caps: "5 GRAMMY NOMINATIONS. I DONT EVEN KNOW WHAT TO SAY. BUT THANK YOU SO MUCH. GREATEST TEAM IN THE WORLD. IT'S BEEN A LOOONNNG TIME COMING! GOD IS GOOD."[11]

The future was bright for this young R&B icon-to-be. The music world had clearly taken notice, and fans couldn't wait to see what she'd produce next. As *Elle* magazine put it, "H.E.R. is more than a rising star—she's a damn galaxy."[12]

# LIVING THE STAR LIFE

After H.E.R.'s Grammy wins, more fans were flocking to her music than ever before. But even for a musician who had been singing in front of an audience since she was a preteen, her increasing fame still required an adjustment. "I've been feeling it more and more lately," H.E.R. told the *Chicago Tribune* in an interview. "At first everything was surreal and kind of like a dream. But after the Grammys I get recognized more—even without my glasses on. People are constantly DM'ing me on social media, hearing my songs on the radio. I mean, even flight attendants are recognizing me!"[1]

To celebrate her star status and Grammy wins, H.E.R. paired up with Childish Gambino, whose song "This Is America" made history for being the first rap song to take home Record of the Year. She played a few shows with Gambino in Europe. On March 24 and 25, 2019, they

Early 2019 brought H.E.R. to the United Kingdom for more awards shows and performances.

"I think the future of R&B is safe with [H.E.R.'s] contribution. Fans resonate with the vibes and emotion her music evokes. Her sound is very right now while still keeping the soulfulness of the R&B we grew up on alive."[3]
—*Grammy-nominated singer-songwriter BJ The Chicago Kid*

## GRAMMY NODS AND R&B

In 1999, Lauryn Hill won Album of the Year for *The Miseducation of Lauryn Hill*. It was the first hip-hop/R&B album to do so. But since then, the Grammys haven't looked favorably on the R&B genre. In 2011, five R&B categories were actually cut from the Grammys, including Best Urban/ Alternative Performance, Best Female R&B Vocal Performance, Best Male R&B Vocal Performance, Best R&B Performance by a Duo or Group with Vocals, and Best Contemporary R&B Album.

performed at London's O2 Arena, followed by a concert at Paris's AccorHotels Arena on March 27. She also made plans to debut a new song at Coachella, a huge outdoor music festival in California, on April 14.

"I'm so thankful for all the stuff that happened in 2018 and now 2019 is even crazier. There's so much going on, so many places that I'll be going to that I haven't seen," she told *Vibe* magazine. "But I'm definitely going to drop an official album, a real album because the projects that I dropped weren't even official. They were just EPs and it's about elevation this year."[2]

H.E.R.'s 2019 performance at Coachella featured new music and dazzling lighting effects.

## ROMANCE VIBES?

In the midst of all the fame and fortune, however, something was missing. Some celebrity couples are pros at discussing their relationship statuses on social media.

But H.E.R.'s fans were scrambling to find out anything they could about her love life—and coming up empty.

In 2016, H.E.R. had vaguely referenced a nasty breakup in interviews, citing it as the inspiration for some of her songs. "I remember saying I'll never be that girl, I'll never be that girl that falls for the wrong guy. I was constantly criticizing that girl and eventually I found myself being that girl, being *her*," she said at the time.

Two years later, she gave an on-air interview with 99 Jamz Radio in Florida. Again, she kept her relationship status vague, even when she was asked about it directly. "I'm living my life, y'know," she said. "We all have a lot of ups and downs—relationships or

## A DIFFERENT KIND OF LOVE

For most of her career, H.E.R. has put romance on the back burner—or at least that's what it seems like to her fans. But on May 6, 2019, she signed on to a project to promote a different sort of love. She took to the stage at The Theatre at the Ace Hotel in downtown Los Angeles as part of VH1's annual Mother's Day celebration. Called *Dear Mama: A Love Letter to Mom*, it featured performances from artists such as Ashanti, Monica, and Luke James. H.E.R. sang Leon Russell's "A Song for You" while playing the piano. Then she gave a shout-out to her mom, who was in the audience. H.E.R. closed her act by calling up Shai, one of her mother's favorite bands. Then she bounded down to her mom's seat and gave her a big hug.

not. Lots of situations, more so than relationships. But I'm just living my life."[4]

Then, in November 2019, H.E.R. uploaded a teaser for a music video on Instagram to promote a new single

**H.E.R. has largely avoided the kind of public relationship drama that has embroiled many other stars.**

called "Slow Down." It was a collaboration with Bob Marley's grandson Skip. Released in January 2020, the video featured an intimate scene in which the two musicians danced closely with each other on a packed dance floor. The lyrics had a romantic feel to them, talking about finding love after waiting for it for a long time.

"It was a natural connection . . . as we met it was just a natural type of vibe between us, it's like we get each other a little bit . . . [H.E.R.] is so down-to-earth, man, she's so cool, she's beautiful."[5]

–*Skip Marley*

**Relationship speculation swirled online between H.E.R. and Skip Marley in 2020.**

Hundreds of fans posted comments about a possible romantic connection. "Modern version of Bob and Lauryn," wrote one. "Umm so why yall not married yet?" wrote another.[6] But neither musician would confirm or deny that they were in an official relationship.

## EMBRACING THE SPOTLIGHT

H.E.R.'s lips were sealed when it came to giving details about her love life to the media and fans. But there was one thing she wasn't shy about anymore: her career and her place in the spotlight. By the summer and through the fall of 2019, she was doing everything she could to attract more fans. For one, after Coachella, she fully embraced the festival circuit. She performed

## A HISTORY-MAKING FESTIVAL

On September 16, 2019, H.E.R. gave a knockout performance at the sold-out inaugural Lights On Festival at the Concord Pavilion in Concord, California. A whopping 14,000 people attended.[7] But that wasn't the only thing that impressed the audience and music critics. She also made history as the curator of the festival. H.E.R.'s event was the first-ever festival owned by a woman of color.

H.E.R. headlined the festival, with special guests DRAM and YBN Cordae. Other acts included Jhené Aiko, Daniel Caesar, Summer Walker, and Ari Lennox. The festival also featured a tent that showed screenings from new filmmakers, a live art installation, interactive tents with live instruments, an R&B museum and guitar lounge, and a big arcade.

at Austin City Limits, Intersect Music Festival, Chicago's Lollapalooza Festival, and the Rock in Rio Festival in Rio de Janeiro, Brazil. She performed at her own festival, the Lights On Festival in Concord, California. She made the rounds on morning and late-night talk shows too, including *The Late Show with Stephen Colbert*, *The Ellen DeGeneres Show*, and others.

Throughout all the public appearances, H.E.R. was also churning out new music. On August 30, she released *I Used to Know Her*, her first full-length compilation. It included 14 songs from *The Prelude* and *Part 2* plus five new ones. The cover featured a photograph of H.E.R. leaning over a younger version of herself playing the guitar.

As with her previous releases, *I Used to Know*

## THE BIG REVEAL

Ever since the first release in 2016, H.E.R. had hidden her face—and sometimes her body—on her EP covers. *H.E.R., Vol. 1* and *Vol. 2* each featured a dark silhouette against a vibrant background. For *I Used to Know Her: The Prelude*, she chose a blurry image of herself holding up an equally blurry photograph. *Part 2* used the same cover image but with a slightly less blurry photograph. But with *I Used to Know Her*, all was revealed. The cover art of the album clearly shows H.E.R. teaching a younger version of herself how to play guitar.

The 2019 Global Citizen Festival, held in New York's Central Park, featured H.E.R. and several other notable artists, including Alicia Keys and Pharrell Williams.

*Her* included songs recorded with other big-name artists, including Bryson Tiller ("Could've Been"), YBN Cordae ("Racks"), and DJ Scratch ("Lost Souls"). Tracks such as "Something Keeps Pulling Me Back" and a live version of a new song called "Uninvited" continued to feature lyrics about romance, breakups, and female empowerment. One of the most uplifting songs on the album was "21."

"I wrote this song when I turned 21," H.E.R. told *Rolling Stone.* "It was one of the best years of my life! I'm experiencing all the things I prayed for as a kid and more. The scary part is, it's just the beginning."[8]

At the end of 2019, H.E.R. was more successful than ever before. She had racked up more award nominations,

**H.E.R. performed in Rio de Janeiro, Brazil, in late 2019.**

> **H.E.R.'s exhilarating performances and increasing critical recognition in 2019 set her up for even greater success in the year to come.**

including for R&B Artist of the Year and Best New R&B Artist at the iHeartRadio Music Awards; Top R&B Artist, Top R&B Female Artist, and Top R&B Album at the Billboard Music Awards; and Best New Artist, Best Push Artist, and Best R&B Song at the MTV Video Music Awards. She also won a BET Her Award for "Hard Place" and Best R&B/Soul Artist at the Soul Train Music Awards.

H.E.R. was sure 2020 would be the year she would officially take the music world by storm. She hoped for more Grammy wins and to develop her passion for acting. But something unforeseen was on the horizon—a life-changing phenomenon that affected not just H.E.R. but the entire world.

# THE SLOW-JAM QUEEN

At the beginning of 2020, the outlook for the coming year in music was promising. In March and April, the SXSW Music Festival in Austin, Texas, and Coachella in Indio, California, were gearing up to host some of the biggest names in music. The performers at these festivals were set to include Frank Ocean, YBN Cordae, Lana Del Ray, Daniel Caesar, Travis Scott, and R&B collective MICHELLE. Hundreds of thousands of fans were expected to attend.

Twenty-two-year-old H.E.R. was up for five Grammys for the second year in a row, including Best R&B Performance and Best R&B Song for "Could've Been," Song of the Year for "Hard Place," Album of the Year for *I Used to Know Her*, and Record of the Year for "Hard Place." Though she didn't take home any awards from the event, she still felt pumped for the year to come. "I did not think

**The Grammys once again recognized H.E.R. in 2020, nominating her for five awards.**

"It's a great thing to hear people putting me up to this standard and putting me on this pedestal and expecting greatness from me, but at the end of the day, I'm just trying to be a better me as an artist musically. As a person, I'm just trying to be better than I was yesterday and continue to elevate."[2]

*—H.E.R.*

the second time I would be nominated for five. That makes it ten nominations in two years, which is kind of unheard of. I feel really special and grateful," she told *Billboard*. "If anything, this is motivation to work harder."[1]

H.E.R. performed with Skip Marley, *left*, at the NAACP Image Awards on February 22, 2020. It would be one of her last live shows before the COVID-19 lockdown.

But something bigger was sweeping not just the nation but the whole world. Appearing in December 2019 in Wuhan, China, and becoming a full-blown crisis by late February 2020, a respiratory disease called COVID-19 was spreading around the world. Governments shut down restaurants and told people to stay home and avoid crowded public spaces to slow the spread of the disease. Theaters and cinemas closed. Concerts, festivals, and live music performances came to a screeching halt. Musicians, including H.E.R., stopped touring or doing in-person events.

Despite the lockdown, H.E.R. did what she could to keep making music. She reached out to her fans whenever possible,

## COVID-19'S IMPACT ON THE MUSIC INDUSTRY

Beginning in 2019 and stretching into 2021, the COVID-19 pandemic had a significant impact on the music industry. Thousands of large and small events across the world were canceled, including festivals, concert tours, and award shows. While some artists were able to create new work from the confines of their homes, many lost their studio spaces, recording studios, and worst of all, a key source of income from live touring. According to a November 2020 report by UK Music, musicians lost approximately two-thirds of their income as a result of COVID-19. Concert trade publication *Pollstar* estimated that the total amount of lost revenue for the live music industry in 2020 was more than $30 billion.[3]

## "GIRLS WITH GUITARS"

On April 6, 2020, H.E.R. launched a weekly series on Instagram called "Girls with Guitars" as a way to interact with her fans. She played live versions of songs from her catalog and took song requests. She also invited other female rockers on to chat and jam, including Sheryl Crow, Melissa Etheridge, Willow Smith, Chloe x Halle, Tori Kelly, Alessia Cara, Lianne La Havas, and Nai Palm (Hiatus Kaiyote).

In June, H.E.R. staged a special Black Music Month edition. Sponsored by RCA Records as part of its "Black Sounds Beautiful" campaign, she had Miguel, Koffee, and A$AP Ferg as musical guests. Proceeds from the show went to the Rock the Vote organization, which sought to increase awareness of voter education and registration for young people.

even under the dire circumstances. Like other musicians, she posted songs and updates on social media. One of her biggest projects landed in April. She launched "Girls with Guitars," a weekly Instagram live performance and conversation series. "In the beginning it was kind of selfish. It was quarantine and I was bored, so I wanted to rock out with other girls who play guitar," she said of the series. "It became a platform for girls who play guitar who are unknown—you know, girls who are just playing in their rooms. So, then it became more of a celebration of girls with guitars."[4]

## PROJECTS GALORE

"Girls with Guitars" was a huge hit with H.E.R.'s fans. But it wasn't the first time she had done something to give back to the community. In 2019, she had established the Bring the Noise Foundation. Its mission was to provide underprivileged students and aspiring musicians with

**H.E.R. appeared on the September 2020 broadcast of the Emmy Awards, performing during the segment memorializing figures in television who had died the previous year.**

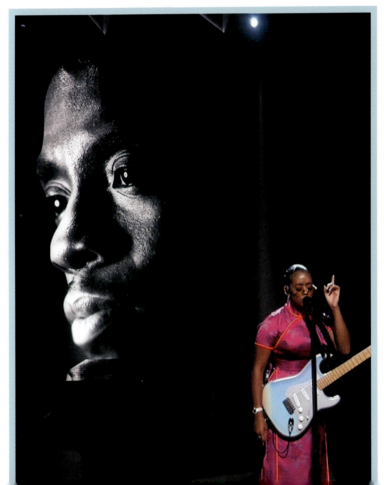

## "I CAN'T BREATHE"

On June 19, 2020, H.E.R. released the song "I Can't Breathe." It was created in response to the May 25 death of George Floyd in police custody in Minneapolis, Minnesota. The officer involved, Derek Chauvin, was later convicted of murder in the case. As soon as the song hit the airwaves, it became known by fans and media outlets alike as the protest song of the summer, a heartrending tribute to Floyd, Breonna Taylor, and countless other Black lives lost at the hands of police.

The song originated in a FaceTime conversation with her cowriter, Tiara Thomas. They were discussing the massive wave of protests popping up around the country and the world in reaction to Floyd's murder. Their words became the lyrics. "I definitely feel a responsibility because I have this platform," H.E.R. said. "But I think we should all speak out against things that we don't like and things that should change, regardless of where we come from. Hate is hate."[6]

access to instruments and instruction. "I plan on donating a bunch of guitars to different schools around the country. There could be a new Slash out there, there could be a new Lenny Kravitz," she told the *New York Post* at the time. "That is really the goal—to inspire little girls to do stuff that may not be expected of them."[5]

H.E.R.'s ventures outside of music have also involved the fashion world. She partnered with luxury brand DIFF Eyewear on a line of sunglasses. She was also recruited by Tommy Hilfiger to help design a fashion collection with acclaimed British race car driver Lewis Hamilton.

The 12-piece series included 100 percent organic cotton T-shirts, a hoodie, lanyards, and a mesh dress. It was a big hit when it was unveiled during London Fashion Week in February 2020.

"We are united in the belief that fashion should be for everyone, so putting inclusivity at the heart of the capsule was a no-brainer," H.E.R. said about the collection. "It was an incredibly creative and collaborative experience, and it was fulfilling to be able to express myself in a fresh way through the medium of fashion."[7]

H.E.R. also made headway in her film career during this period. She snagged a cameo in the movie *Yes Day*, which released in March 2021. She also worked on a number of soundtracks for movies, including *The Photograph*, *Waves*, and *All Day and a Night*, as well as the TV series *13 Reasons Why* and *Council of Dads*.

## A BRIGHT FUTURE

For the 23-year-old musician whom the *Guardian* nicknamed "the slow-jam queen," the future was looking bright in mid-2021.[8] H.E.R.'s tour schedule was on hold because of restrictions related to COVID-19. Still, she was hard at work on a library of new music, with hundreds of new songs ready to go, according to her dad.

Though most music venues remained closed to the public at this time, H.E.R. also took part in music-related events whenever possible. On February 7, slinging her signature Fender Stratocaster, she sang a rendition of "America the Beautiful" at the Super Bowl to the delight of 100 million at-home viewers.[9] She picked up a Best Original Song nomination at the Golden Globe Awards and won her first Oscar, for Best Original Song, for the song "Fight for You" from the motion picture *Judas and the Black Messiah*. She also took home two more Grammys, bringing her total up to four. She won Best R&B Song

**H.E.R.'s Super Bowl performance represented by far her biggest stage yet.**

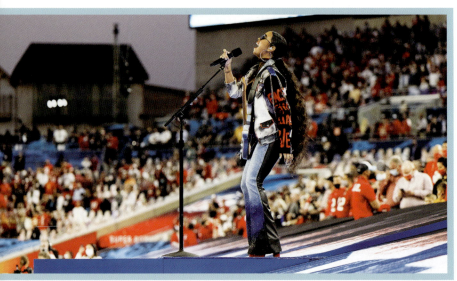

**H.E.R. picked up her first career Oscar at the Academy Awards ceremony in Los Angeles in April 2021.**

for "Better Than I Imagined" and Song of the Year for "I Can't Breathe."

Without a doubt, H.E.R. has made her mark on the music industry. She has brought R&B to new heights, attracting millions of fans to her soulful, sultry music. Those fans were excited to see what she would do next. In April 2021, she announced she would finally release her first official full-length album that summer. The album, titled *Back of My Mind*, came out in June. It received favorable reviews from critics, with British music publication *NME* calling the album "a victory lap after a stellar start to the year."[10]

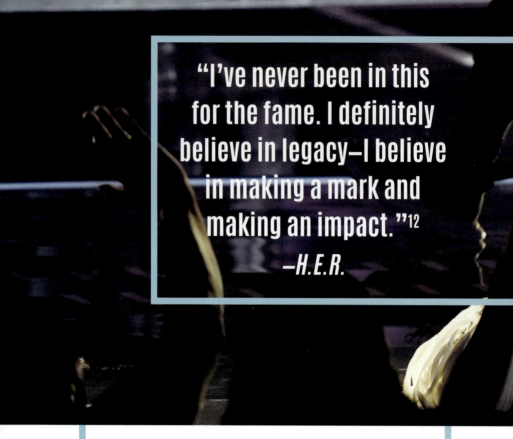

"I've never been in this for the fame. I definitely believe in legacy—I believe in making a mark and making an impact."[12]

–H.E.R.

H.E.R. gave a dramatic performance at the BET Awards in June 2021.

Whatever the future holds, H.E.R. is up for the challenge. "At this point I have no doubts about the future because everything has worked out so perfectly until now. And even when it didn't seem like it was working out it

was always going to work out in the end," she told the *Chicago Tribune*. "I'm one of the highly favored, I guess you could say."[11]

## TIMELINE

**1997**

Gabriella (Gabi) Wilson is born on June 27 in Vallejo, California.

**2007**

Gabi performs on a number of high-profile shows, including *Showtime at the Apollo*.

**2009**

Gabi performs at the 22nd Annual Rhythm & Soul Music Awards on June 26.

Starting on September 23, Gabi competes on Radio Disney's *Next Big Thing*; she also lands a role in Nick Cannon's made-for-TV movie *School Gyrls*.

**2010**

On her birthday, Gabi performs an a cappella rendition of verses from Alicia Keys's "Fallin'" at the BET Awards.

**2014**

Gabi signs a contract with RCA Records/Sony Entertainment and releases a debut single titled "Something to Prove." Then she disappears from the music world's radar for two years.

**2016**

In September, a new R&B artist releases her debut EP, called *H.E.R., Vol. 1*; a music reporter identifies H.E.R. as Gabi Wilson.

**2017**

H.E.R. releases a second EP, called *H.E.R., Vol. 2*, on June 16; to promote the album, she joins Bryson Tiller on his Set It Off tour.

In November, H.E.R. embarks on her first headlining tour, called the Lights On tour.

## 2018

On August 3, H.E.R. releases *I Used to Know Her: The Prelude*, followed by *I Used to Know Her: Part 2* on November 2.

H.E.R. lands seven 2018 Soul Train Music Award nominations, winning one for Best Collaboration Performance ("Best Part") and another for Best Album/Mix-Tape (*H.E.R.*).

## 2019

H.E.R. is nominated for five Grammys and wins Best R&B Song for "Best Part" and Best R&B Album of the Year for *H.E.R.*

H.E.R. plays at a number of festivals, including Coachella, Austin City Limits, and Lollapalooza; she debuts her own festival, the Lights On Festival.

On August 30, H.E.R. releases *I Used to Know Her*, her first full-length compilation.

## 2020

The COVID-19 pandemic spreads to countries around the world, closing music venues.

In April, H.E.R. creates "Girls with Guitars," a weekly Instagram live performance and conversation series.

## 2021

H.E.R. performs "America the Beautiful" at the Super Bowl on February 7.

H.E.R. wins an Oscar and two Grammys.

In June, H.E.R.'s first full-length album, *Back of My Mind*, is released.

### FULL NAME

Gabriella Sarmiento Wilson (H.E.R.)

### DATE OF BIRTH

June 27, 1997

### PLACE OF BIRTH

Vallejo, California

### PARENTS

Agnes Wilson and Kenny Wilson

### EDUCATION

North Hills Christian School, Rodriguez High School

### CAREER HIGHLIGHTS

With one full-length album and seven EPs under her belt, H.E.R. has earned a lot of accolades. She was nominated for five Grammys two years in a row, winning four of the trophies. She won her first Oscar in 2021, for Best Original Song, for "Fight for You," which was from the movie *Judas and the Black Messiah*. In addition to receiving many other awards, she sang at the Super Bowl, appeared on *Saturday Night Live*, and has pioneered her own fashion lines. H.E.R. has also given back to the community. She created "Girls with Guitars," a weekly Instagram live performance and conversation series to raise money for Rock the Vote. Her song "I Can't Breathe" became a rallying cry for protestors who were speaking out against police brutality after the killing of George Floyd.

## EPs, COMPILATIONS, AND ALBUMS

*H.E.R., Vol. 1* (EP, 2016), *H.E.R., Vol. 2* (EP, 2017), *H.E.R., Vol. 2: The B-Sides* (EP, 2017), *H.E.R.* (compilation, 2017), *I Used to Know Her: The Prelude* (EP, 2018), *I Used to Know Her: Part 2* (EP, 2018), *I Used to Know Her* (compilation, 2019), *Back of My Mind* (album, 2021)

## CONTRIBUTION TO HIP-HOP

Within a few years of releasing her first EP in 2016, H.E.R. took the R&B music world by storm. Fans adore her revealing songs about love, heartache, sex, and female empowerment. By singing about her most personal struggles, she opened the door for others to write more sensitive lyrics. In a historically misogynistic industry, she also encouraged fans and media alike to focus not on her looks and her figure but on her lyrics and talent instead.

## CONFLICTS

For a famous R&B star, H.E.R. hasn't gotten into much trouble during her career. She hasn't struggled with drug or alcohol addiction, nor has she been in trouble with the law. She hasn't had a feud with a fellow musician, as some artists do. Perhaps the closest she has come to conflict is to hide her true identity from the public when she introduced herself to the music world as H.E.R.

## QUOTE

"As a young woman, I experienced high school and heartbreak, and the music I started to write was a little bit more poetic. . . . The real raw emotional things that sit in the back of our minds, that you were afraid to say? That's how I started to write my music."

—*H.E.R.*

## ANONYMOUS

Not named or identified.

## DEBUT

The first appearance, often of an album or publication, made by a musician or group.

## EXTENDED PLAY (EP)

A musical recording of several songs, longer than a single but shorter than an album.

## INAUGURAL

Related to the beginning of something or the first of its kind.

## JAM SESSION

An informal gathering of musicians who play and improvise songs together.

## LINER NOTES

Biographical or song-related information included with CDs or records or attached to digital recordings.

## MIXTAPE

A compilation of unreleased tracks, freestyle rap music, and DJ mixes of songs.

## PLATINUM

An award, given by the Recording Industry Association of America (RIAA), that represents huge sales—500,000 albums for gold, one million for platinum, and two million or more for multiplatinum.

## PREDECESSOR

A person or thing that came before or has been replaced by another.

## PRESTIGIOUS

Inspiring respect and admiration; having high status.

## R&B

Rhythm and blues; a type of pop music of African American origin that has a soulful vocal style and features improvisation.

## RENDITION

A version of something.

## SHRED

To skillfully play the guitar.

## SILHOUETTE

The outline or general shape of something.

## SPECULATIVE

Based on a guess and not on factual information.

## TRACK

A song or piece of music recorded onto a physical medium.

## SELECTED BIBLIOGRAPHY

Janes, DeAnna. "Who Is H.E.R.? Everything to Know about Oscar Winner Gabi Wilson." *Oprah Daily*, 26 Apr. 2021, oprahdaily.com. Accessed 21 May 2021.

Pasori, Cedar. "Mysterious R&B Singer H.E.R. Already Has a Fan in Rihanna." *Interview*, 4 Jan. 2018, interviewmagazine.com. Accessed 21 May 2021.

Thompson, Desire. "21 Reasons to Love H.E.R." *Vibe*, 9 Feb. 2019, vibe.com. Accessed 21 May 2021.

## FURTHER READINGS

DeAngelis, Audrey. *Cardi B: Groundbreaking Rap Powerhouse*. Abdo, 2020.

Kallen, Stuart A. *Careers in Music*. ReferencePoint, 2020.

Murray, Laura K. *Childish Gambino: Multifaceted Artist*. Abdo, 2020.

## ONLINE RESOURCES

**Booklinks**
**NONFICTION NETWORK**
FREE! ONLINE NONFICTION RESOURCES

To learn more about H.E.R., please visit **abdobooklinks.com** or scan this QR code. These links are routinely monitored and updated to provide the most current information available.

## MORE INFORMATION

For more information on this subject, contact or visit the following organizations:

**GRAMMY MUSEUM**
800 W. Olympic Blvd.
Los Angeles, CA 90015-1300
213-725-5700
grammymuseum.org

Founded in 2008, this museum in downtown Los Angeles has exhibits on four floors that cover many aspects of the music business, including the recording process and the history of the Grammy Awards. It also features rotating exhibits about famous musicians.

**NATIONAL MUSEUM OF AFRICAN AMERICAN MUSIC**
510 Broadway
Nashville, TN 37203
615-301-8724
nmaam.org

The National Museum of African American Music is the only museum dedicated to preserving and celebrating the many music genres created, influenced, and inspired by African Americans. The interactive exhibits contain more than 1,600 artifacts, including one of Ella Fitzgerald's Grammy Awards and a guitar owned by B. B. King.

## SOURCE NOTES

### CHAPTER 1. A NIGHT TO REMEMBER

1. Gerrick D. Kennedy. "H.E.R. Went from Child Star to Enigmatic R&B Sensation—On Her Terms." *Los Angeles Times*, 16 Dec. 2018, latimes.com. Accessed 3 Aug. 2021.

2. Maeve McDermott. "Grammys 2019 Predictions: Who Will Win the Night's Biggest Awards and Who Should." *USA Today*, 10 Feb. 2019, usatoday.com. Accessed 3 Aug. 2021.

3. Maggie Griswold. "H.E.R.'s Shiny Grammys Power Suit Is Exactly as Cool as She Is." *StyleCaster*, 10 Feb. 2019, stylecaster.com. Accessed 3 Aug. 2021.

4. "H.E.R. Red Carpet Interview (2019 Grammys)." *YouTube*, uploaded by Recording Academy / Grammys, 10 Feb. 2019, youtube.com. Accessed 3 Aug. 2021.

5. "H.E.R. Red Carpet Interview."

6. Mike Duffy. "Artists Break Out Fender Gems at 2019 Grammy Awards." *Fender*, n.d., fender.com. Accessed 3 Aug. 2021.

7. "H.E.R. One-on-One Interview." *YouTube*, uploaded by Recording Academy / Grammys, 10 Feb. 2019, youtube.com. Accessed 3 Aug. 2021.

8. Madeline Roth. "H.E.R.'s Guitar-Shredding Grammy Performance Was a Hell of a Debut." *MTV*, 10 Feb. 2019, mtv.com. Accessed 3 Aug. 2021.

9. Roth, "H.E.R.'s Guitar-Shredding Grammy Performance."

10. "H.E.R. TV & Radio Room Interview (2019 Grammys)." *YouTube*, uploaded by Recording Academy / Grammys, 12 Feb. 2019, youtube.com. Accessed 3 Aug. 2021.

11. Kennedy, "H.E.R. Went from Child Star to Enigmatic R&B Sensation."

### CHAPTER 2. CHILD PRODIGY

1. Sydney Gore. "H.E.R. Is Fully Focused on Maintaining Control of Her Truest Self." *Highsnobiety*, n.d., highsnobiety.com. Accessed 3 Aug. 2021

2. Maxine Wally. "H.E.R. Finally Reveals All: The Identity, the History, and the Future." *WWD*, 27 Aug. 2018, wwd.com. Accessed 3 Aug. 2021.

3. "Urban Bushmen Band." *Urban Bushmen*, n.d., urbanbushmen.com. Accessed 3 Aug. 2021.

4. "Showtime at the Apollo." *Vallejo Times Herald*, 31 Aug. 2007, timesheraldonline.com. Accessed 3 Aug. 2021.

5. "Showtime at the Apollo."

6. "Showtime at the Apollo."

7. Mike Celizic. "Music Prodigy, 10, Attracting a Lot of Attention." *Today*, 19 Dec. 2007, today.com. Accessed 3 Aug. 2021.

8. "Showtime at the Apollo."

9. "Is This America's Most Talented Kid?" *Today*, 4 Dec. 2007, today.com. Accessed 3 Aug. 2021.

### CHAPTER 3. AMERICA'S "NEXT BIG THING"

1. Rich Freedman. "Vallejo's Gabi Wilson Gets the Red-Carpet Treatment." *Vallejo Times Herald*, 15 Aug. 2016, eastbaytimes.com. Accessed 3 Aug. 2021.

2. "H.E.R. (Gabi Wilson) 12 Years Old – Radio Disney." *YouTube*, uploaded by Pete Alexander, 24 Sept. 2009, youtube.com. Accessed 3 Aug. 2021.

3. "Gabi Wilson Is One to Watch in 2014." *Nick Cannon*, 30 Dec. 2013, nickcannon.com. Accessed 3 Aug. 2021.

4. Kenny Wardell. "Gabi Wilson Shines at 17." *BAM Magazine*, 15 Nov. 2014, bammagazine.com. Accessed 3 Aug. 2021.

5. Mesfin Fekadu. "Doing It H.E.R. Way: Singer Gabi Wilson Emerges from Shadows." *NBC Connecticut*, 7 Nov. 2018, nbcconnecticut.com. Accessed 3 Aug. 2021.

6. "Gabi Wilson Is One to Watch."

## CHAPTER 4. WHO IS H.E.R.?

1. Lauren Nostro. "Here's the Secret Identity of H.E.R., the Mysterious Singer Signed to RCA Records." *Genius*, 13 Sept. 2016, genius.com. Accessed 3 Aug. 2021.

2. @aliciakeys. "Have you heard @HERMusicx yet? #vibes." *Twitter*, 12 Sept. 2016, 1:59 p.m., twitter.com. Accessed 3 Aug. 2021.

3. Niki McGloster. "H.E.R. Reigns As One of the Year's Lowkey R&B MVPs." *Billboard*, 23 Dec. 2016. billboard.com. Accessed 3 Aug. 2021.

4. Stacy-Ann Ellis. "Review: Cloaked Artists Are Annoying, but 'H.E.R. Volume 1' Proved That Sometimes Not Knowing Is Best." *Vibe*, 30 Sept. 2016, vibe.com. Accessed 3 Aug. 2021.

5. Ellis, "Review."

6. Brian Hiatt. "H.E.R. on Her Rise, Her Influences and Her Future." *Rolling Stone*, 30 Dec. 2019, rollingstone.com. Accessed 3 Aug. 2021.

7. Nostro, "Here's the Secret Identity of H.E.R."

8. Nostro, "Here's the Secret Identity of H.E.R."

9. Ogden Payne. "5 Alternative R&B Artists to Look Out For in 2017." *Forbes*, n.d., forbes.com. Accessed 3 Aug. 2021.

10. Lauren Nostro. "Premiere: Listen to Gabi Wilson's Stunning Cover of Drake's 'Jungle.'" *Complex*, 5 Mar. 2015, complex.com. Accessed 3 Aug. 2021.

11. Bobby Carter and Kiana Fitzgerald. "5 Essential R&B Albums You Slept On in 2016." *NPR Music*, 17 Dec. 2016, npr.com. Accessed 3 Aug. 2021.

## CHAPTER 5. THE RISE TO FAME

1. Niki McGloster. "H.E.R. Reigns As One of the Year's Lowkey R&B MVPs." *Billboard*, 23 Dec. 2016, billboard.com. Accessed 3 Aug. 2021.

2. Gerrick D. Kennedy. "H.E.R. Went from Child Star to Enigmatic R&B Sensation—On Her Terms." *Los Angeles Times*, 16 Dec. 2018, latimes.com. Accessed 3 Aug. 2021.

3. Sydney Gore. "H.E.R. Is Fully Focused on Maintaining Control of Her Truest Self." *Highsnobiety*, n.d., highsnobiety.com. Accessed 3 Aug. 2021.

4. Briana Younger. "H.E.R. Vol. 2 EP." *Pitchfork*, 23 Jun. 2017, pitchfork.com. Accessed 3 Aug. 2021.

5. Desire Thompson. "21 Reasons to Love H.E.R." *Vibe*, 9 Feb. 2019, vibe.com. Accessed 3 Aug. 2021.

6. D-Money. "H.E.R. Gets Closer to Revealing Herself On 'H.E.R. Vol. 2.'" *SoulBounce*, 16 Jun. 2017, soulbounce.com. Accessed 3 Aug. 2021.

7. "H.E.R. Releases Official Music Video For 'Every Kind Of Way' and New Song '2' From 'H.E.R. Vol. 2: The B Sides.'" *RCA Records*, 13 Oct. 2017, rcarecords.com. Accessed 3 Aug. 2021.

8. Ashley Lyle. "The World Finally Gets a Glimpse of H.E.R. During 2017 BET Experience." *Billboard*, 24 Jun. 2017, billboard.com. Accessed 3 Aug. 2021.

9. Lyle, "The World Finally Gets a Glimpse."

SOURCE NOTES

10. Cedar Pasori. "Mysterious R&B Singer H.E.R. Already Has a Fan in Rihanna." *Interview Magazine*, 4 Jan. 2018, interviewmagazine.com. Accessed 3 Aug. 2021.

11. Pasori, "Mysterious R&B Singer H.E.R."

CHAPTER 6. H.E.R.'S FIRST WIN

1. @janetjackson. Photo of H.E.R. and Janet Jackson. *Instagram*, 10 Mar. 2018, instagram.com.

2. Steven J. Horowitz. "H.E.R. Is 'Finally Coming Into My Own'—And Ready to Conquer This Fall." *Billboard*, 13 Sept. 2018, billboard.com. Accessed 3 Aug. 2021.

3. Sydney Gore. "H.E.R. Is Fully Focused on Maintaining Control of Her Truest Self." *Highsnobiety*, n.d., highsnobiety.com. Accessed 3 Aug. 2021.

4. Cristina Jerome. "R&B Fans Struggled to Live Their Best Lives at Best Life Festival." *Miami New Times*, 16 Sept. 2018, miaminewtimes.com. Accessed 3 Aug. 2021.

5. Summer Holmes. "H.E.R. Prepares For Debut Album With 'I Used To Know Her: The Prelude' EP." *NPR Music*, 3 Aug. 2018, npr.com. Accessed 3 Aug. 2021.

6. Gerrick D. Kennedy. "H.E.R. Went from Child Star to Enigmatic R&B Sensation—On Her Terms." *Los Angeles Times*, 16 Dec. 2018, latimes.com. Accessed 3 Aug. 2021.

7. Richard Freedman. "Gabi Wilson—Now H.E.R. —Makes 'Tonight Show' Debut." *Vallejo Times Herald*, 8 Oct. 2018, timesheraldonline.com. Accessed 3 Aug. 2021.

8. Gore, "H.E.R. Is Fully Focused."

9. Antwane Folk. "H.E.R. Scores First Gold Record with 'Focus' + Readies 'I Used to Know Her: Part 2' EP." *Rated R&B*, 30 Oct. 2018, ratedrnb.com. Accessed 3 Aug. 2021.

10. "Gold Platinum: H.E.R." *Recording Industry Association of America*, n.d., riaa.com. Accessed 3 Aug. 2021.

11. Brianne Tracy. "Meet 5-Time 2019 Grammy Nominee H.E.R.! What to Know About the Singer Up for Best New Artist." *People*, 7 Dec. 2018, people.com. Accessed 3 Aug. 2021.

12. Kristina Rodulfo. "H.E.R. Is More Than a Rising Star—She's A Damn Galaxy." *Elle*, 21 Sept. 2018, elle.com. Accessed 3 Aug. 2021.

CHAPTER 7. LIVING THE STAR LIFE

1. Dan Hyman. "H.E.R. Is Living Up to the Outsized Hype that First Greeted Gabi Wilson's Hitting the Scene." *Chicago Tribune*, 25 Jul. 2019, chicagotribune.com. Accessed 3 Aug. 2021.

2. Desire Thompson. "21 Reasons to Love H.E.R." *Vibe*, 9 Feb. 2019, vibe.com. Accessed 3 Aug. 2021.

3. Thompson, "21 Reasons."

4. Sade Spence. "H.E.R.'s Relationship Status Is Just As Mysterious As Her Persona." *Elite Daily*, 22 Jan. 2020, elitedaily.com. Accessed 3 Aug. 2021.

5. D.L. Thompson. "Is H.E.R. Dating Skip Marley? Is He Her Boyfriend?" *Heavy*, 7 Feb. 2021, heavy.com. Accessed 3 Aug. 2021.

6. @hermusicofficial. "Clip of 'Slow Down' music video." *Instagram*, 3 Jan. 2020, instagram.com.

7. "Grammy Award Winner H.E.R. Lit Up the Bay Area with Her Sold-Out 'Lights On Festival' This Weekend." *RCA Records*, 16 Sept. 2019, rcarecords.com. Accessed 3 Aug. 2021.

8. Claire Shaffer. "See H.E.R. Celebrate Her Whirlwind Year in '21' Video." *Rolling Stone*, 26 Jul. 2019, rollingstone.com. Accessed 3 Aug. 2021.

## CHAPTER 8. THE SLOW-JAM QUEEN

1. Joe Lynch. "H.E.R. on 5 Grammy Nominations: 'If Anything, This Is Motivation to Work Harder.' *Billboard*, 20 Nov. 2021, billboard.com. Accessed 3 Aug. 2021.

2. Desire Thompson. "21 Reasons to Love H.E.R." *Vibe*, 9 Feb. 2019, vibe.com. Accessed 3 Aug. 2021.

3. Mesfin Fekadu. "Pollstar: Live Events Industry Cost $30B Due to Pandemic." *AP*, 11 Dec. 2020, apnews.com. Accessed 3 Aug. 2021.

4. Nick Levine. "H.E.R.: 'I Definitely Feel a Responsibility to Use My Platform. We Should All Speak Out Against Things That We Don't Like.'" *NME*, 30 Apr. 2021, nme.com. Accessed 3 Aug. 2021.

5. Chuck Arnold. "H.E.R. Out to Prove She Earned Her Grammys with New Concert." *New York Post,* 9 May 2019, nypost.com. Accessed 3 Aug. 2021.

6. Levine, "H.E.R.: 'I Definitely Feel a Responsibility.'"

7. Nerisha Penrose. "Tommy Hilfiger and Lewis Hamilton Launch Surprise Collection with H.E.R." *Elle*, 12 Feb. 2020, elle.com. Accessed 3 Aug. 2021.

8. Leonie Cooper. "R&B Star H.E.R.: 'I Wanted to Be Anonymous.'" *Guardian*, 5 Nov. 2018, theguardian.com. Accessed 3 Aug. 2021.

9. Richard Freedman. "February 18 Arts and Entertainment Source: H.E.R. Fame More Than Dad Saw Coming." *Vallejo Times Herald*, 16 Feb. 2021, timesheraldonline.com. Accessed 3 Aug. 2021.

10. Nick Levine. "H.E.R. – 'Back Of My Mind' Review: A Victory Lap After a Stellar Start to the Year." *NME*, 18 Jun. 2021, nme.com. Accessed 3 Aug. 2021.

11. Dan Hyman. "H.E.R. Is Living Up to the Outsized Hype that First Greeted Gabi Wilson's Hitting the Scene." *Chicago Tribune*, 25 Jul. 2019, chicagotribune.com. Accessed 3 Aug. 2021.

12. Levine, "H.E.R.: 'I Definitely Feel a Responsibility.'"

# INDEX

ABOUT THE *AUTHOR*

## DORIS EDWARDS

Doris Edwards lives in Portland, Oregon. She has written many books for teens and young readers. When she isn't writing, you can find her gardening or practicing the fiddle on her back porch.